D1035311

DISCARD

Artist's Studio

Dance

by Jenny Fretland VanVoorst

Bullfrog
Books

Ideas for Parents and Teachers

Bullfrog Books let children practice reading informational text at the earliest reading levels. Repetition, familiar words, and photo labels support early readers.

Before Reading

- Discuss the cover photo. What does it tell them?
- Look at the picture glossary together. Read and discuss the words.

Read the Book

- "Walk" through the book and look at the photos. Let the child ask questions. Point out the photo labels.
- Read the book to the child, or have him or her read independently.

After Reading

- Prompt the child to think more. Ask: Do you like to dance? Is there a style of dancing you like best?

Bullfrog Books are published by Jump!
5357 Penn Avenue South
Minneapolis, MN 55419
www.jumplibrary.com

Copyright © 2016 Jump! International copyright reserved in all countries. No part of this book may be reproduced in any form without written permission from the publisher.

Library of Congress Cataloging-in-Publication Data

Fretland VanVoorst, Jenny, 1972–
  Dance / by Jenny Fretland VanVoorst.
     pages cm. — (Artist's studio)
  Includes index.
  ISBN 978-1-62031-281-0 (hardcover: alk. paper) —
  ISBN 978-1-62496-241-4 (ebook)
  1. Dance—Juvenile literature. I. Title.
  GV1596.5.F74 2016
  792.8—dc23
                                              2015022430

Series Designer: Ellen Huber
Book Designer: Michelle Sonnek
Photo Researcher: Michelle Sonnek

Photo Credits: All photos by Shutterstock except:
David Shackleford/Oakland Breakerz, 12–13, 14–15,
16, 18–19; iStock, 22br; Jack.Q/Shutterstock.com, 5,
6, 8–9, 10–11; SuperStock, 20–21.

Printed in the United States of America at
Corporate Graphics in North Mankato, Minnesota.

RO451824891

Table of Contents

Let's Dance!

Gail is a dancer.

She uses her body
to tell a story.

She dances with others.
She is part of a company.

6

She wears special shoes.

They let her dance on her toes.

Gail stands on one leg.
Her partner holds her.
She twirls.

Look at her body.

What story is it telling?

Kev is a dancer, too.

He dances
on the street.

He puts down
some cardboard.

It makes a good
surface for dancing.

cardboard

He moves like a robot.

He spins.

16

People stop to watch.
They clap. They cheer.

17

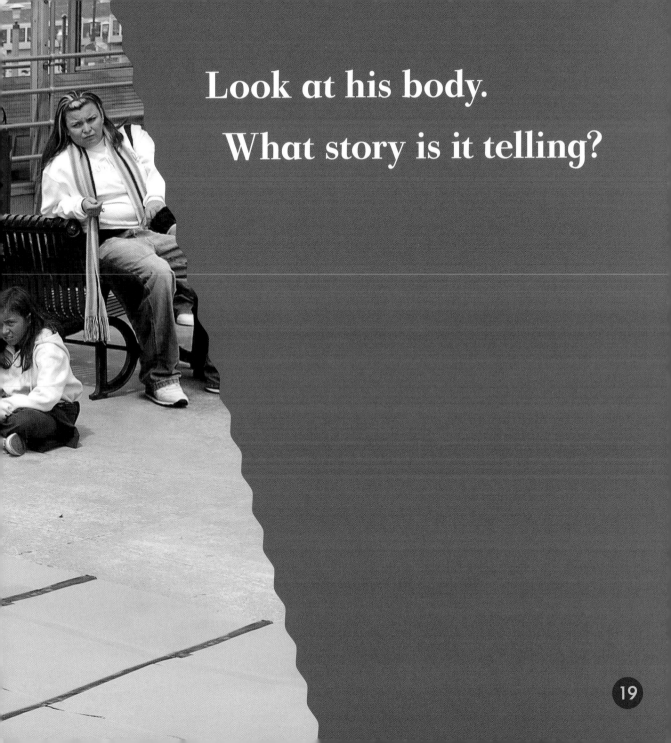

Look at his body.

What story is it telling?

Try it yourself!
Dancing is fun.

Dancing Shoes

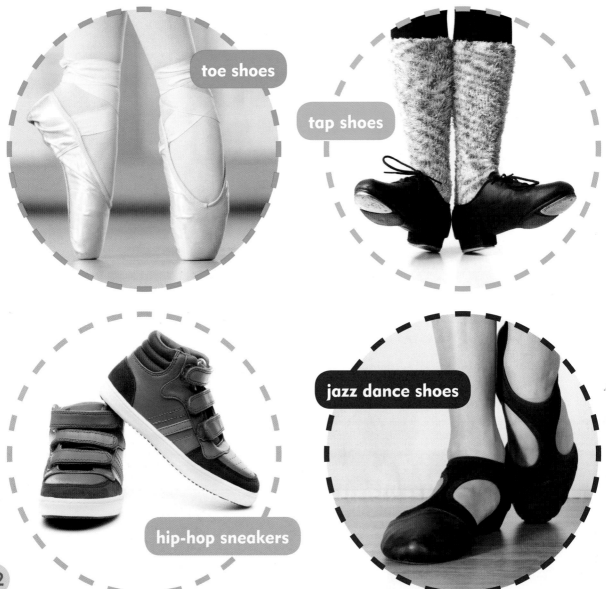

toe shoes

tap shoes

hip-hop sneakers

jazz dance shoes

Picture Glossary

cardboard
A material made from wood pulp that is like paper only thicker.

partner
Either member of a couple who dance together.

company
An organized group of performers.

surface
The outermost layer of something.

23

Index

To Learn More

Learning more is as easy as 1, 2, 3.

1) Go to www.factsurfer.com

2) Enter "dance" into the search box.

3) Click the "Surf" button to see a list of websites.

With factsurfer.com, finding more information is just a click away.